W9-DEW-604

DISASTER ZONE
VOLCANOES

by Cari Meister

pogo

Ideas for Parents and Teachers

Pogo Books let children practice reading informational text while introducing them to nonfiction features such as headings, labels, sidebars, maps, and diagrams, as well as a table of contents, glossary, and index.

Carefully leveled text with a strong photo match offers early fluent readers the support they need to succeed.

Before Reading

- "Walk" through the book and point out the various nonfiction features. Ask the student what purpose each feature serves.
- Look at the glossary together. Read and discuss the words.

Read the Book

- Have the child read the book independently.
- Invite him or her to list questions that arise from reading.

After Reading

- Discuss the child's questions. Talk about how he or she might find answers to those questions.
- Prompt the child to think more. Ask: Have you ever been anywhere where there's been a volcano?

Pogo Books are published by Jump!
5357 Penn Avenue South
Minneapolis, MN 55419
www.jumplibrary.com

Library of Congress Cataloging-in-Publication Data

Meister, Cari, author.
  Volcanoes / by Cari Meister.
      pages cm – (Disaster zone)
  Audience: Ages 7-10.
  Includes bibliographical references and index.
  ISBN 978-1-62031-227-8 (hardcover: alk. paper) –
  ISBN 978-1-62031-270-4 (paperback) –
  ISBN 978-1-62496-314-8 (ebook)
  1. Volcanoes–Juvenile literature. I. Title.
  QE521.3.M454 2016
  551.21–dc23

                                    2014047063

Series Editor: Jenny Fretland VanVoorst
Series Designer: Anna Peterson
Photo Researcher: Anna Peterson

Photo Credits: All photos by Shutterstock except: Alamy, 8-9; Corbis, 1, 5, 16, 17, 20-21; Thinkstock, 4, 14-15.

Printed in the United States of America at Corporate Graphics in North Mankato, Minnesota.

TABLE OF CONTENTS

CHAPTER 1

. . . .

WHAT IS A VOLCANO?

Imagine you are on a boat on Lake Arenal in Costa Rica. In the distance you see ash coming out of a mountain. A river of rock flows down its side.

Wow! It's a volcano!

Volcanoes are **vents** in the earth's surface. They let out gas, rocks, **lava**, and ash into the air.

Some **eruptions** last for days, slowly oozing lava. Others are quick and violent. They throw lava and ash high in the air.

What causes a volcano to erupt?

North American
Plate

Eurasian
Plate

The earth's **crust** is made up of plates. They fit together like a puzzle. The plates move on a bed of hot, liquid rock. They bump against each other.

The liquid rock is called **magma**. Sometimes magma is pushed up through a hole in the crust. When it comes out, it is called lava.

TAKE A LOOK!

In a volcano, magma inside the earth is forced to the surface.

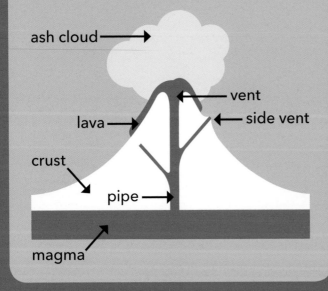

ash cloud →

vent ←

lava →

side vent ←

crust ↘

pipe →

magma ↗

CHAPTER 2

· ·

WHAT AND WHERE?

When you think of a volcano, you probably think of a **composite volcano**. They are tall and steep.

composite volcano

shield
volcano

But some volcanoes are short and wide. They are **shield volcanoes**.

There are about 1,900 active volcanoes in the world. Most are near the edges of the earth's plates. Ninety percent are in an area called the **Ring of Fire**.

WHERE IS IT?

The Ring of Fire is in the Pacific Ocean. It is an area where many plates come together.

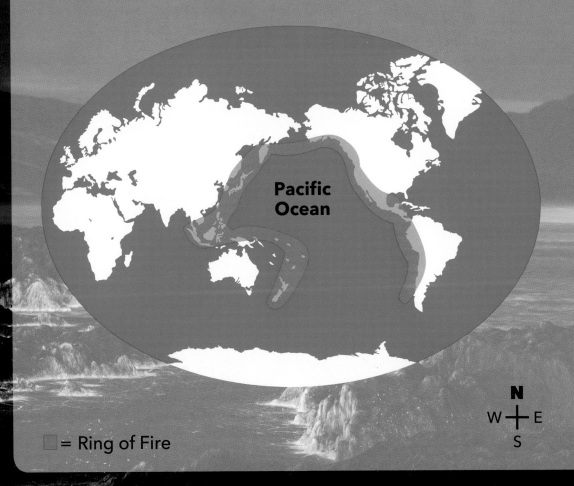

Pacific Ocean

N
W E
S

☐ = Ring of Fire

CHAPTER 3

. . . .

DEADLY VOLCANOES

Volcanoes can be deadly. Lava gets hot enough to melt glass. Gases are harmful to breathe.

◄····· **harmful gases**

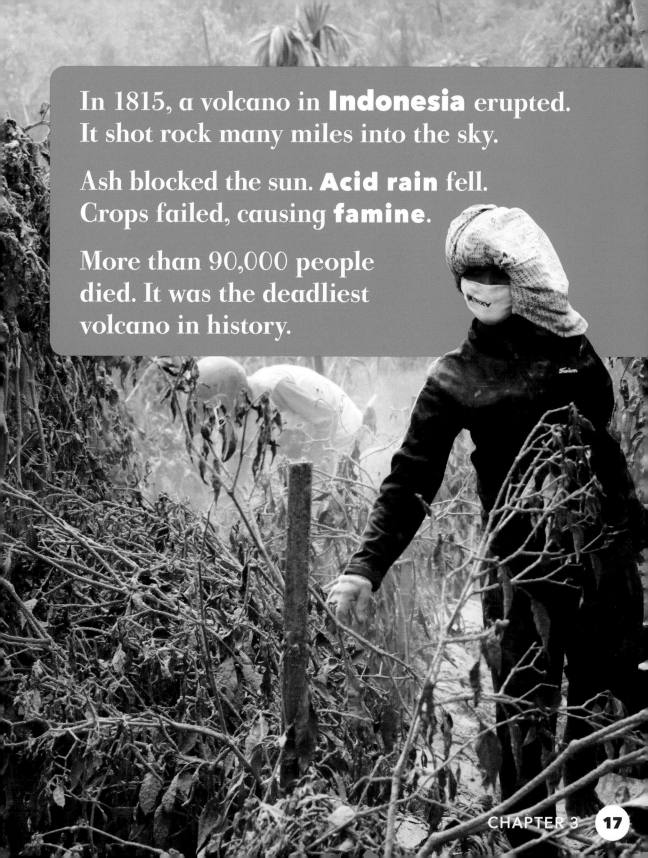

In 1815, a volcano in **Indonesia** erupted. It shot rock many miles into the sky.

Ash blocked the sun. **Acid rain** fell. Crops failed, causing **famine**.

More than 90,000 people died. It was the deadliest volcano in history.

In 79 B.C.E., Mount Vesuvius in Italy erupted. Ash covered the entire city of Pompeii. It preserved the city. This let scientists see what life was like at that time and place.

Mount
Vesuvius

Today scientists can recognize signs that a volcano will erupt. So listen to local officials.

Disasters can happen anytime. But be prepared, and you can stay safe when a volcano erupts.

DID YOU KNOW?

An emergency kit is helpful in any disaster. It should include:

- Water
- Canned or dried food (and a can opener)
- First aid kit
- Cell phone and charger
- Radio
- Blankets

ACTIVITIES & TOOLS

VOLCANO IN A BOTTLE

What You Need:

- glue
- large sheet of cardboard
- 2 plastic bottles
- 6 cups (1.4 liters) of flour
- 2 cups (.5 l) of salt
- ½ cup (120 milliliters) of vinegar
- 3 drops dish soap
- 3 drops red and/or orange food coloring
- paint and paintbrush
- 3 tbsp. (45 ml) baking soda

1. Glue the bottom of a plastic bottle to the middle of the cardboard.

2. Mix the flour and salt with one cup of water to form a clay.

3. Pack the wet clay around the bottle to make a cone shape.

4. Let the clay dry for 24 hours, and then paint it to look like a volcano.

5. When the paint is dry, combine the vinegar, dish soap, and food coloring in the second plastic bottle, and shake to mix.

6. Pour the mixture into your volcano.

7. Add the baking soda and watch your volcano erupt!

GLOSSARY

acid rain: Rain that has been made acidic by pollution or environmental causes.

composite volcano: A type of volcano with tall, steep sides.

crust: The top layer of the earth.

dormant: Inactive or "sleeping;" volcanoes that are dormant may erupt again in the future.

eruption: A forceful explosion of rocks, hot ashes, and lava.

famine: A period during which food is scarce and people starve.

Indonesia: A country in Southeast Asia made up of thousands of islands.

lava: Hot, liquid rock that comes out of a volcano.

magma: Hot, liquid rock inside the earth.

shield volcano: A type of volcano that has short, wide sides.

vents: Holes in the earth's crust.

INDEX

TO LEARN MORE

Learning more is as easy as 1, 2, 3.

1) **Go to www.factsurfer.com**

2) **Enter "volcanoes" into the search box.**

3) **Click the "Surf" to see a list of websites.**

With factsurfer, finding more information is just a click away.